Advance Praise for
Not Enough, Too Much

Andrea Hernández Holm's work embodies the healing and insight that can only come from a life lived in close relationship with el desierto y su cultura fronteriza. This book is for anyone who needs to "poem their way home."

—**Logan Phillips**, author of *Sonoran Strange*

Andrea Hernández Holm's *Not Enough, Too Much* is a revelation of affirmations and "not enough's" for what Gloria Anzaldúa calls the border culture: Hernández Holm's interrogation of her Chicana, Mestiza, and American identities is healing and devastation—a blood that never stills. To pray for looking at the skies the way her ancestors have, to turn towards the weeping heavens as angels walk away, to pine for a harvest that doesn't speak of her grandfather's labor: these are the refrains of an attention that honors one's gratitude and pushback to epistolary pain. Hernández Holm is a blood that never stops.

—**Sylvia Chan**, author of *We Remain Traditional*

Not Enough, Too Much, Andrea Hernández Holm's first poetry collection, reads like an exquisite map of the Chicana heart. Each poem a witness to family, the body, how she celebrates and grieves, and, more importantly, how the Chicana heart moves in life and beyond always in the company of her ancestors.

—**Mari Herreras**, author of *At Grande* and *Congress*

Dipping into a sensitive arroyo where splattering images of memory, loss, love and hope flow simultaneously, Andrea Hernández Holm has brought forth poetic offerings that demand reading and rereading. She has found a creative way to mesh often unutterable tear-stained longings with delicate, celebratory occasions, presenting them in beautiful phrasing, which allows honesty and thriving to surface.

—**MariJo Moore**, author of *11 Conjured Stories*

Not Enough, Too Much

FLOWERSONG
PRESS

poetry by

Andrea Hernández Holm

FLOWERSONG
PRESS

For my beautiful, strong, and loving family.

With all my love to Garett.

Acknowledgements

Many thanks to the community of writers that has welcomed, encouraged, and uplifted me. There are so many people who are in my heart. I am forever grateful to the comadres of Sowing the Seeds, especially Elena Díaz Björkquist, Rosi Andrade, and Mari Herreras; the community of Poets Responding and Francisco X. Alarcón and Odilia Galván Rodriguez; and Michael Sedano and his Online Floricanto at LaBloga. I would also like to thank author Denise Chávez, whose words— "We're waiting for you and your poems"-- have always stayed with me and kept me moving when I've wanted to stop.

- "My Total Sum." In *Somos Xicanas* (Somos en escrito Literary Foundation Press. 2024.
- "Fat Mexican." In *Power of Storm*, edited by Marijo Moore. Renegade Planets Publishing. 2020.
- "Sacred Migrations." In *Anacua Literary Arts Journal: Migrations*. 2020.
- "Not Enough, Too Much." 2012. La Bloga, www.labloga. blogspot.com. 2012.
- "Angels in Arizona." La Bloga, www.labloga.blogspot. com. 2011.
- "Birth." In "Floating Borderlands: Chicanas and Mexicanas Moving Knowledge in the Borderlands." Diss., The University of Arizona, 2016; In *Our Spirit,*

Our Reality, edited by Elena Díaz Bjorkquist and Rosi Andrade. Wheatmark Press, 2011.

- "Harvest Time in Pinal County." La Bloga, www.labloga. blogspot.com. 2011.

- "In Response to the Man Who Asked, "Why do your people march for everything?" *In Poetry as Resistance*, edited by Francisco X. Alarcón and Odilia Galván Rodriguez. University of Arizona Press. 2015.

table of contents

Not Enough,
Too Much

Gordita

She is not burdened
by the weight she carries.
In fact, her pounds are wings,
That lift her up
so that she merely glides
over the ground,
toes touching earth lightly
as she enters a room and fills it.

She is vibrant.

Words jingle on her tongue
and in the folds of her skirt
as she sashays through time
collecting our stories,
tucking them in sleeves,
behind her ear,
between her breasts
and finally
eating them
to keep them safe.

Thoughts about Migration

We are a migrating people
who rise with the dawn
to follow the sun
wherever he may lead us.

We are carried by the breath
of the universe
among the flowers and the trees
over seas and into deep canyons.

We walk forth from the corn,
we walk forth from the belly,
we walk,
we walk,
we walk.

We walk
together.

Not Enough, Too Much

I must be
some kind of illegal
poet
crossing borders
with words
that reveal
not enough
Chicana
not enough
Spanish
not enough
of everything

broken
Spanglish
del este lado
between identities
and dreams
my truth
too much
Mestiza
too much
Indigena
too much
and nothing

Border poem in motion

I am the dirt in your bones
The grit in your teeth
A translated dream
From somewhere in between

Border Identity Disorder

To be
of *el otro lado,*
this side,
and in-between
all at the same time;
to not know what *el otro lado*
means
but to feel it in your bones;
to dream in ancestral tongues
and wake in English
always English;
to be the hyphen
in your own identity.

Birth

I did not swim into the world
in a river of amniotic fluid
but in a steady stream of stories
sustained by mí abuelita, mí mama, y mís tias.
They nourished me with their words,
tales of grandmothers passed,
places loved,
and times gone by.

On Sunday afternoons
we crowded into Abuelita's room,
where I curled in a dark corner,
quiet
while these women, my women,
pulled memories
from the old leather petaquilla.

Each took a corner
and together, unfolded
stories like quilts--
spread them out
and shook
the dust and wrinkles away.

They placed one memory upon another
until I lay under the blanket of our history,
warm and content in its embrace.

When the petaquilla was empty,
the words spread about us
like drifts and dunes near the sea.
 And it was these women
who listened for my breathing
and with great ease,
brought me to light.

Uninvited grandmother
(*mulatta libre*, 1783 Marriage Record)

She would not have invited
the binding of her hands—
they were likely clamped in steel cuffs
perhaps linked by chains
to other women of the household,
maybe her sisters or cousins,
their fates inextricably joined
as they journeyed across seas and deserts
arriving unannounced and uninvited
in the Chihuahua highlands.
There was no invitation issued for her wedding
to the *apachi* man who himself
was a servant, a man indentured.
There was only the testimony offered by
four *dons* who were entrusted with the affirmation
of her freedom to marry.
But she invites me now
across centuries and miles and languages
to understand how her story is my story.
Holding her hands out open,
she invites me now.

That's my hair

That's my hair
you're brushing.
I can feel my scalp
tingle
as you draw the bristles
through it over and over.

That's my hair
and my abuelita's hair,
and her abuelita's hair
you're brushing,
pulled out across
centuries and oceans
and deserts,
spirals of our ancestry.

That's my hair,
wild and curly
and everywhere.
It doesn't want to be coifed or
combed or curbed.
It doesn't want to be managed,
I don't want to be managed.

I want to be windswept
I want to be myself
I want to be free.

Como celebrar el 16 de septiembre

Necesito una map
to get me to the homelands *de mis Mexicanos.*
Necesito un interpreter
por que hablo solamente un poquito español
y mas malo tambien.
I don't speak Raramuri or Nahuatl at all.
Necesito a quick lesson in the rosary
so that I may pray to la Virgen de Guadalupe
to protect me on my way.

Necesito the permission of two governments
to cross the border
even though *mis antepasados*
were here, and there,
before there was a border.

Necesito estar donde mis parientes estaban,
a mirar el cielo como lo hicieron
to understand their love for their Mexico
and let it become my own.

Pero lo unico que tengo son
mis palabras rotas
calabacitas
nopalitos

frijoles
tortillas de maiz,
momentos de intenso dolor,
lagrimas de agradecimiento,
y una fotografia
de la princesa de la independencia,
la hija del pueblo.

Mother tongues

The ancestors will know you
no matter what language you speak/don't speak.
Don't worry.
They will recognize you
when you call out to them.
They will hear you
and gather to greet you.

Cycles

I keep writing
About the same things
The same dreams
The water dreams
The laughing
The abuelitas
The memories
I keep writing about
Food
Water
Dreams
Languages
Memories
      Mine
      Theirs
      Shared
Desert dreams
Water words
Warrior words
Language tastes
Ancestors
Abuelos
Ancestral water
Ancestral dreams

Whispers
Memories
     Mine
     Theirs
     Me

Why is writing a poem so hard?

I know poetry
>	I've eaten 100 poems
>	And let their flavor tantalize my taste buds
>	And imagination long into the night

I know what poems sound like, feel like, look like
>	I can close my eyes and see
>	Words darting through darkness

Slamming into one another
United in power
And they form some great poems
Some dare I say
>	Bomb
>	Ass
>	Poems

Poems that cross borders
Erase borders
Consume borders

My poems become paths
Between the ancestors and me
Raramuri memories
Nahuatl nouns Tex-Mex ingredients
Arizona sunsets and that
>	Deep
>	Musky

Creosote chapparal guame
That rises from the desert with rain

So why is writing a poem so hard?
Because it comes from within
It comes from my heart
And my soul
A poem comes from some
Way back abuelitos
And yet it finds me
The poem finds its way through time
And space and life
And death
It sneaks into dreams and memories
It leaks through tears and laughter
It does what it has to do to find me
Because it is waiting to be written, wanting
To be written and it will not
Make the moment of its emergence easy.

It has too much to do in this world.

Hard because survival is hard
And resiliency is hard
And just being here is hard.

But
    We
        Do
           IT.

Today I celebrated Columbus Day

Today I celebrated being here
to hear the songs of the drum
to look at my children
and see our ancestors and our future
to breathe and be
despite Columbus/because of Columbus.

A dia de los muertos

She asked
why build an altar
for the *antepasados*?
They know they're dead.

And her heart clenched
so the tears wouldn't flow
because missing them and
missing everything about how life
used to be was too much
too hard to face.
To build an altar
even a tiny one--
a singular candle,
a singular flower,
a singular memory.

Abuela in the Dawn

Rise at dawn
before the hours
wrap themselves around you.

Rise at dawn
to find the wood your sons stacked
so you can feed it to the stove
in the front yard.

Rise at dawn and wait.

Pull the masa round and round
Into reflections of the fading moon.

Rise at dawn
to feed your children
who will carry you in their hearts
long after the cancer has bound your body
and set your spirit free.

Abuelo in Montana

In Montana you pulled apples swiftly,
rescued them from a rapid descent
to the earth below.
You breathed easy then--
your lungs let air in
captured life and saved it for later,
when disease blocked its entrance.

In Montana you watched your sons grow
into men who worked hard
by your side
who caress your memory now
like fruit to be harvested for someone else.

You were theirs in Montana.
You belonged to them
even as you labored for others.

Angels and Arizona

1.
Turn, open your eyes
See the angels falling
Pummeled in mid-flight
By invisible fists
Knuckles
That must have been beaten raw
By frantic wings

2.
Turn, arch your neck
So you may see the top of the wall
And watch the angels
Break under the weight
Of a young man
Plummeting to the desert floor

3. Turn, quickly
And you will see a child
Who the angels stole
From a world that did not deserve her.

4. Turn, listen closely

So you can hear the heavens weeping

As the angels turn their backs and walk away

Annual Vistors, *Dia de los Muertos*

They will come sailing in today
on cool November breezes
for one more taste of earthly sweets.

They remember us, know where to find us.

My heart is always full
of their love.

Susto

He grew up sleeping side by side with brothers;
learned to breathe and be with them and
listened to stiletto rain dances on *lamina* rooftops.
He held hands with sisters,
pressed soft palms lightly against calloused ones.

He traveled highways, backways, and farm roads;
looked ahead, looked out
for the fields and orchards to be picked.
Always with his brothers,
always with his father, and
always returning,
to the little house with a broken window
and his mother's woodstove in the front yard.

When the Army took him,
he sent photos of snow covered mountain tops,
unfamiliar faces,
and the barracks where he lived
separated for the first time
from the warmth of his brothers nearby.

He won't talk about what it was like over there.
Or what it was like to come back here.

Some people do not return whole.
Their spirits fracture and float away,
never again feeling quite right
or fitting where they once belonged.

Being Arizona

On slow desert mornings
like today,
I offer my face to the sun
while his kisses are warm,
still gentle.
I feed him with the tears
I seem to cry every day now
and offer him pieces of my broken heart.
I patiently, quietly
sing my prayers
send them up and out,
hoping and encouraging myself to believe
if not in the spirit world,
if not in the ancestors,
if not in myself,
in the possibility of tomorrow.

In Response to the Man Who Asked, "Why do your people march for everything?"

We were marching long before
We even knew how to walk,
Before there was a notion of you or me—
Just a hope that there would be
One more generation of our people,
And another after that.

Our nanas marched us out of their wombs
To the rhythm of the drum
And we kept on marching, walking
Dancing, and singing
Until our praises were carried
In all directions
So that our ancestors would know we were here.

We march
Through sorrow and joy.
We march
When we are happy
And when we are angry.
We have marched from the belly of the earth
Through the deserts and mountains and rivers,
In the canyons and forests,

By the moonlight and the sunlight,
In the rain and the snow and the heat.

You can see the pattern of our journey
In the stars above.

We march until our voices are too weak
To sing us further.
We march until we are heavy with sweat.
We march to exhaustion.
We march until we bleed,
And still we march.

We make sense of the universe
When we march.
The pounding of our feet reverberates,
Returns to the life force
In all that surrounds us.

We do not march for ourselves.
We are only bodies of energy,
Our lives are but brief moments in time.
We march in the hope that there will be
One more generation of our people
And another after that.

Poets Responding

They carry me
Wrapped securely upon their backs
Bound bone to bone upon their backs
They carry me
When I think I cannot think
Anymore
Or hurt
Anymore
Or dream
Anymore
They carry me
Use their words as shields
Use their words as salve
Use their words
To carry me.

Disappearing

By pressing the tip of my finger
flat against the map
I can make the entire border region disappear.
I can disappear the disappeared,
damaged, and broken
bones that lie
below the desert sand.

Everywhere from
Nogales // Nogales
            to
El Paso // Juarez
will suffocate under the pressure.

Centennial sentiments

the one-hundredth anniversary of statehood

Arizona was not born in 1912.
It did not come forth from the womb
of the U.S. government,
or the Mexican government,
or the Spanish crown before that.
Arizona was already here
and the people were born from it
long before 1912.

Cross-cultural communications

I just want to tell you,
you shouldn't wake me
when I'm sleeping.
Because it
it might startle me.
It might startle me
and my *tonalli* will get lost,
and my *tonalli* won't be able
to come back.

How
will
your
tah-mah-li
get lost?

No,
not
tamal--

Sorry--
tamal

tonalli.

You're not listening.

No-pah-li?

Tonalli.
It's my
Spirit.

Your

Tonalli

Tonalli.
Your
Mexican

Nahua

spirit.

Yes.

Okay.

Woman in the desert

They say the heart of the home
is the hearth,
the formidable source of warmth
where we rest to rejuvenate
to heal
to restore ourselves before
going out into the world again--
like the heart of a woman
--standing fierce against all odds
The center
and the origin
of hope.

Daughter's obligations

She would sit by your side,
hold your hand in hers
stroke your dry skin,
lovingly note
the rise and fall of your chest
as you tried
to hold on to breath.
Her tears would fall
upon your cheek
as she watched
your body quake.

She would, I know she would
love you until the very end,
until your soul decided
it was time to leave
to stretch in the sunlight
toward something better
younger, fresher, new.

She would stand at your edge
and smile as you disappeared
into the distance.

She is your mother
my mother

our mother,
so we will sit by her side.

Together we will hold her
and mourn her thirst
and we will call upon the sky
to give her rain.
We will plant our feet
and hold steady.
We will gather
together with the elk
and the buffalo, the rabbits,
the birds, and the spiders
so that she will know our voices.
So that she will know that we are here
and that we remember.

Day 23

Sometimes
there really are no words
sad enough or loving enough
to capture what I want to say
so I offer that which remains constant:
an open heart
an open face
arms open
and wide,
my whole body
full of prayers and hope.

Dear Andrea

When I think of you I see your eyes
     As dark as moonless nights
When I think of you I hear children running
     As loud as a herd of horses
When I think of you I smell tobacco
     As deeply roasted as monsoon earth
When I think of you I feel
     As lonely as desert flowers
When I think of you I imagine
     The comforting warmth of campfire.

Recipe for reunion

Take a plate down from the cupboard
Gently
Because it belonged
To one of the *bisabuelas*
And has survived
The many years and miles
Between mothers and daughters.

Dust it gingerly with the washcloth
Embroidered by a *tia*,
Its small yellow daisies
Worn by use.

Scoop the first serving
From each bowl holding tonight's dinner,
Generously
As *familia* is always hungry
(Don't forget the *té*).

Kindly place it
To the west
As that is the direction
From which we'll come

Annual remembering

In November,
I was married in the desert,
blessed by the presence of family and friends.
The sun was kind to us that day,
kissing us gently as
we were promised to one another
and our families were bound together,
a reunification of our people.

There was a meteor shower
on my wedding night.
We were told.
"Your ancestors are having a party up there."

December 12
The Feast Day of *Nuestra Señora de Guadalupe*

Every day is sacred,
another opportunity to breathe and be,
but some days feel more significant than others.

While prayers flicker across our lips,
candles dance in homes and churches
throughout the Americas and around the world.

We remember Our Guadalupe—
mostly the gentleness we want to hold on to,
the fierceness in her love, and her promise
to stand between us and harm.

In her honor, we feast on hope
and savor the promise that we survive.

Growing Up

You don't know
what it's like
to want God
until you no longer have a mother,
she said.

And my heart stopped
in that flat space--
that moment in the early hours
when the sunlight slides in;
that burning sensation
when tears gather;
that whisper
where words float
without purpose--
that I fear most.

Guadalupe Trail

We arrive in Albuquerque
ushered in by my own crying
because I cannot lean against my mother's shoulder here
or hold my nieces' baby hands here.

When the tears stop
and the rain begins
     the rain always comforts me
I know I must find something.

I find the road.
Curiosity and devotion,
compel me to follow it
and I drive in
curves
circles
curses
around million dollar homes
(next door to million year old casitas).

Cottonwoods drop soft blossoms
and I see.

Yes, there she is. *Nuestra Señora de Guadalupe*
carved into the trunk of a cottonwood,
aged but not fading, candles at her feet.

Each day I head out again.
My toddler in the back seat asks, "Where's Guadalupe?,"
knowing we'll find her
because every day, she waits to welcome us home.

Godless Goddess

I have a
Godless goddess,
a sculptress   a poet
who crafts life
because she can:
a hoarder
of hearts and tongues.

I should rise

I should
wake up with the sun,
rise as the stars recede
with the darkness.
I should
greet the world
with the loving embrace
my parents taught me.

Long ago,
when it was easy to be
loving
and welcoming,
when it was easy to be
awed
by the beauty and magnificence
of the morning light
carried on the wings
of hummingbirds and butterflies,
I would
offer my thanks
and acknowledge
the blessing
of another day.

Even when I know
that day may offer
sadness and fear
for some of us, or all of us,
I should rise with the sun,
be the center of my own universe
and revel in the warmth
of my own magnitude.

To those who made the journey this year

I will say goodbye again to you tonight,
send my words and tears out on the candles' flames.
You brought music and laughter to my life
because you loved to sing and dance.
And I loved you for it.

I will celebrate you tonight,
offer stories and songs about you in my dreams.
You gave me the saguaro's fruits
and I loved you for it.

I will remember you tonight,
pray for all of us with the sweet scents of sage.

I will miss you tonight
and always.

Just let go

Just let go
Breathe deep in
Breathe deep out
And let it all…go.

I wish I could.
I wish my heart could
blink away the memory
of hurt
and anger
and it would all float away,
tattered dreams
getting smaller and smaller
as they float away.

Letting go

You can't leave my mom's house
without a blessing. She doesn't make
the sign of the cross
anymore and sometimes, she doesn't
even say the prayers out loud
but she catches you before you leave,
holds you close and you know,
> *May God bless you and keep you safe.*
> *Every time. All the time. Always.*
> *Que dios te bendiga su viaje*

I send my sons to school alone
and am tempted to keep them home
where I can see them and kiss them
and talk with them any time I want.
I can make taquitos for lunch and
we can watch movies in the afternoon.
I bought a cake mix, we could bake that for dessert.
If I keep them home, I can hear them laugh and fight
and breathe.

I let them go.

But not without a prayer first, you know
May God bless you and keep you safe.
Every time. All the time. Always.

How do prayers find us?

I lay under a heavy blanket of calm created by ceremony
and wonder about the prayers sent up and the energies received.

I wonder about distances between now and the places that we
come from.

How do my prayers find their destinations?

Does the destination reside in me? In the earth? In all of us or
nothing?

Loyalties

Margarita would rise at 4 am to make tortillas
even though there were no troops to feed
after her eleven children were grown
and most of her grandchildren
had gone away too, asleep in their own houses
where she could not hear them toss and turn
in the dark.

Margarita did these things to fill her day:
make tortillas, *panasitos, sopa de arroz con pollo,*
frijoles, fideos, and *chicharrones;*
Watch one *telenovela;*
Sew quilts, *camisas,* other *cositas*
and one pillow
that was red, white, and blue on one side
and red, white, and green on the other.

Husbands and fathers

My small hand fits right inside my dad's hand.
I listen as he tells me, pointing to the sky
about the rabbit in the moon.

> The rabbit in the moon
> watches us always. All the time,
> for a long, long time.

He tells me it's a blessing.

And I remember this much later
when we dance below the moon
on my wedding night.

I remember that he said
> on your wedding night
> the ancestors will come out
> in droves.
> The ancestors will dance
> all together in the night sky.
> in celebration of your love.

And I remember this,
every time the moon waxes,

every time my husband holds me close.
Every time, all the time, always,
ours is a love to celebrate.

Para Papa Al Ruiz

Let the sweet smoke carry our prayers
and you

        you are loved
        and longed for
        and missed

away, into the next world,
where our love will become sweet memories,
morsels for your spirit
until we meet again.
until we meet again.
You are loved
and longed for
and missed.

Poem my way

I'm going to poem my way
Into war
Let the words be my weapons
And armor.

I'm going to poem my way
Into healing
Let the words be my stitches
And salve.

I'm going to poem my way
I'm going to poem my way
I'm going to poem my way home.

Standing up

In the morning we will rise,
the sun and I,
and we will meet the day
while the chill of the night
and the complexities of history
still lie heavy on our bones.

I will draw my breath
he will embrace the sky
and we will pray together
thanks for this, another day
to love and hate,
to taste and see,
to smell and feel,
to live and breathe.

We will pray together
for healing
for the soul wounds
and the body wounds,
the sorrow and the pain
of a thousand years
and more.

We will pray together,
the sun and I,
for each soul
for each person
for loved ones
and for enemies
because we are all one
and need our creator's breath.
On this, our day of thanks,
we will rise,
the sun and I.

Fall ceremonies

Equinox, *dia de los muertos*,
the approaching new year-
this is the time we sweep and clean.

This is the time we perform those *limpias;*
refresh and rejuvenate; and
inhale the healing breath of the universe.

This is the time our elders remind us
> *Open your heart to welcome strength and blessing.*
> *We need it.*

This is the time we ask for love and prayers
for those on their way to the next world,
and peace for those of us they leave behind.

Sweet Nothings

You cast shadows on the surface of my soul.
Your movement, soft,
flutters
and becomes ripples in time.
With the motion of your midnight dances
you sweep the boundaries between us away
and in the fragile threads of a dream
I bear the weight of your bones on my flesh.

In the morning I will offer you light
and sweet fruit, sweet bread, sweet candies
because I know you long for them on the other side.
I will come to you
with your favorite flowers in my hair.
I will sing a farewell to you--
a song to carry you home.
and when I gaze into the night sky
I will watch the stars blink
and I will miss you.

New Year

The cervix of the universe stretches wide
open enough for the new year
to come forth
without witness
because you and I are too busy
celebrating
or sleeping
or hiding
or simply being ignorant.
In this midnight moment
days lie scattered across the earth
drowning in tears shed by the *abuelitos*
as they weep not for time lost
but for you and me.
The days have been born without ceremony
and the songs for their welcome
left among the stars.
The elders pity us
our arrogance
and ignorance
and step forward to set things right.
They gather the days
in their warm and loving hands
bind them

and bless them
for us.

Will we be able to do the same
for our children?

This is what I learn

We were born
From the sun
From the son
From the earth
From the mother
We have come to light
We have known
We have forgotten
We have remembered
We belong
In love
In respect
In peace
Because we were born
For this time
And this place

This is what I learn
From my parents who learned
From their parents who learned
From theirs
In the kitchens
In the gardens
In all the spaces

Where parents teach children
How to be
Who to be
And why.

This is what I learn:
We are not invisible
I am not invisible
Though someone may not envision me;
We are not disposable
I am not disposable
Though someone may wish to throw me away;
We are not despicable
I am not despicable
Though someone may despise me.
This is what I learn:
We were born
I was born
For the sun.
For the son.
For the earth.
For the mother.
And we belong
I belong
In love
In respect
In peace.

Thursday

I don't love you
with diamonds
or roses
or fancy dinners
at restaurants
with dress codes.

I love you
praying in the kitchen
calling First Man
and First Woman
to protect our son
and then taking him outside
to play a quick game of football
before dinner.

Warrior approaching

I hear the ancient
            tsh-tsh-tsh-tsh-tsh
in his voice
behind the young man façade,
            you know, the bravado
            that only teenage boys
            can swagger.
Behind that,
below that,
I hear the ancient
            movement
            that stirs deep within
his heart,
his bones, and
his spirit that cries today
for another spirit.
Good boy.

The Poem I'm Not Writing

I'm not writing poetry
even though I could use a verse
that stretches back in time
weeks   months   centuries
to fill an open wound
with healing words.

To stitch it closed tight
I need a poem to write me.

I need a poem
to carry me on its back
because my hopes buckled
and my sense of direction
points nowhere.

I need an ancestor poem
to recognize me
and hold me close.

I need a poem to right me.

Harvest time in Pinal County

I remember walking
Walking alongside my mother
My sisters so small still,
Me so small still,
And looking up, up, up
At the saguaro arms
Stretched high above us
Straight into the blue sky
Fat, juicy fruit perched on their very tops.
The sound of the fruit
Dropping into our clutches
Like drumbeats
Heartbeats in the desert,
In the foothills of Table Top
Where the doves and quails
Greeted us
And our thanks floated away easily
On occasional breezes.

At the base of Table Top mountain
Today
The Neo-Nazis zoom across the delicate desert
On the backs of ATVs.
Their weapons of assault are draped across their shoulders
Hung low on their hips

Tucked into combat boots
And festering on the tips of their tongues.
The state would pay them
To harvest all the migrants they can find.

We are afraid
To go where we were welcome
Where the desert was kind to us
And let us love it back.

Harvesting the Future

I could have been born
from my Abuelita›s garden,
the one at el Rancho
where the whole family
helped
till the soil
plant the seeds
pull worms off leaves
and lecture the ants away;
they would have nurtured me
like they watered,
like they talked quietly to the sprouts
like they encouraged even the tiniest
spark of green to flourish.
I could have been
the fresh young life
they praised God for delivering
to sustain them.

In the high deserts of Chihuahua, Mexico

In the melancholy of my sleep
I have breathed the thin air
high above the ground,
where—in memories disguised as dreams--
I have run
along canyons and ravines.

As I let the universe carry me forward
I see in the corner of my eye
bright yellow discs,
the center of the sun
and the suggestion of flowers
I don't mean to crush with the arch of my foot.

I follow you along narrow trails
that course like veins
and carry us like blood
to the heart of the earth.

As if by magic
I am tied to you.
every footfall of yours
is one of mine
and as my flesh touches the dirt and rocks
where your flesh once stepped,

I am made whole again
healed by your being
of the lies and hypocrisies
of my waking world.

In the winter of my life
I will close my eyes
and remember the air
above the mountains of our homelands,
a sweet desert taste, and
the sound of our feet pounding
as we run together.

Sacred Migrations

We are in a sacred time
When lines between worlds
Have been worried thin by our weeping
Waiting for dear ones to return
Waiting for a blink
A flutter
In our hearts that tells us they are here
Still with us.

A sacred time
When there is no time.
When we feel angel's wings beat against our backs
And welcome death as it comes
Because we've invited it.

We are in a sacred time
Waiting for ancestors marching across the heavens,
The echo of their footsteps reverberating below
In the march across continents.
All our relatives
Coming
Coming
Coming
To see us and be us
In this sacred time

When the lines between worlds blur
When the lines between life and death blur
We wait with open hearts
Worried thin by our weeping.

I tremble
In the face of the unknown
For only a moment.

There is nothing more sacred
Than movement
The movement across time
Across lines
Across life
Across death.
Movement becomes motion
Trembles become tremors
And the universe splits open
Exposing all our pain and sorrows
All our love and beauty.

The return will bring balance.

The entirety of where I belong

Almost invisible to the eye
Webs reach from the heavens
Entwine us
Tie us to the spirits
So we may not wander
They may not wander
From our mother's side
Above

I am afraid
That Earth may not recognize in my voice
The prayer songs of *mis abuelos*
Where they cared for Her with love
Or know the gentleness of my heart
Where my *abuelita's ombligo* awaits
Within

We grow like the corn grows,
Like the cotton grows,
Tall and strong from the earth
To be picked by the leathery
Brown hands of our mothers
Below

Unexpected warriors rise gently
Brace themselves
Against the world
For me

Hummingbird heart beating
To the rhythm of a war song
Dancing in the sky
Always watching
Always listening for the cry
Of a revolution

Go east
Towards the beloved ones
Let their songs
Draw you into the embrace
Of the morning

My total sum

My elders transition peacefully
with prayers of *God willing* on their lips
and our songs carrying their hearts.
The stories of how we came to be go with them.
The last embrace of the bisabuelos,
Chihuahua on their skin,
and words and songs and laughter that built us—
these ways of us go with them.
We can only keep what we make room for.
Hundred-year old photos of family;
the Rio Bravo--
both sides, in it, on it, with it;
long memories;
rural desert landscapes;
tortillas and nopales;
just snippets.

I struggle.

Who are you? Where do you come from?

Always the same questions.

I try to find my way through
fragments, dreams, and longings

for ways to navigate
these questions.
Are you, am I
north   west   south   east?
Are you, am I
in the homelands?
Are you, am I
the homelands?
Am I
Chicana   Latina   Mexicana
(add x @ e to everything;
insert   remove   insert a hyphen;
silence the visibly invisible accent; align
Raramurí or Mexica or *other;*
layer the Arizona earth
and the monsoon scent,
carry the generations
x y z;
multiply parent, spouse, child, and sibling
and divide it all by home;
add home, subtract home;
arrive at zero,
the ancestral center
where I am everything
and nothing)?

And what does that mean?
What does any of it mean?
The same fears
the same dreams

water dreams
abuela dreams
language dreams
snake dreams;
the same longing
to remember
to replace
to restore
to tell you that
my ancestors wove me into being,
pulled my story
from yarns reaching back through time,
across milpas,
and deserts,
and canyons ,
and dry dusty roads between
cotton fields and cottonwoods,
through stars and mud
to give me light.
To love me
To love me
To love me.

That's it.
That's all I am.

Fat Mexican

I don't have any dainty
Slender
Slim
Parts
No willowy
Wispy
Slip or whisper here.
I am knotted curls
Thick thighs
Flat wide feet
Plump heavy lips,
And heart.
Every part of me
Holds the earth
And knows it.
So call me fat
No me importa
I know I'm full
And fulfilled.

About the Author

Andrea Hernández Holm was raised in central Arizona, surrounded by cotton farms and the Sonoran desert. Her family originated in Northern Mexico and Texas and their stories migrated with them through the U.S.-Mexico Borderlands. Andrea is a desert storyteller, poet, and scholar. She was a 2014 featured poet of the Stjukshon Indigenous reading series at Casa Libre en la Solana. Most recently, her poems have appeared in *Power of the Storm: Indigenous Voices, Visions, and Determination*, *Anacua Literary Arts Journal: Migrations*, *Caja de Resistencia: Revista de poesía crítica,* and *Soñadores—We Came to Dream.* She lives in Tucson with her husband and sons, and is blessed to be near family and friends.

FLOWERSONG
PRESS

FlowerSong Press nurtures essential verse
from, about, and throughout the borderlands.
Literary. Lyrical. Boundless.

Sign up for announcements about
new and upcoming titles at:

www.flowersongpress.com